RETRO ANXIETY

COLORING BOOK

BY ART LOCO

TEST COLOR PAGE

THANK YOU FOR PURCHASING OUR COLORING BOOK! WE
HOPE YOU ENJOY COLORING THE PAGES AND IT BRINGS
YOU JOY. IF YOU LIKE THIS BOOK, WE WOULD GREATLY
APPRECIATE IF YOU COULD TAKE A MOMENT TO LEAVE
AN HONEST REVIEW ON AMAZON.

YOUR FEEDBACK HELPS OTHERS DISCOVER OUR BOOKS
AND IS SO IMPORTANT FOR INDEPENDENT CREATORS
LIKE US. WE READ EACH REVIEW CAREFULLY AND VALUE
YOUR THOUGHTS IN SHAPING OUR FUTURE PRODUCTS.

HAPPY COLORING!

QUICK TIP - PLACE A SHEET OF PAPER UNDERNEATH THE PAGE YOU'RE
COLORING TO STOP MARKER INK FROM BLEEDING THROUGH TO THE
NEXT PAGE.

iN MY
ANXie-TEA
ERA

It's Okay if the Only Thing You Do Today is Breathe

No Drama
Please

NEWS FLASH
Other people's opinions are not your problem.

WTF is Going On in Here

Be kind or else

i'm tired of being nice

On the verge of tears but first coffee

ANTi DEPRESSANTS

JUST
PEACHY

SORRY, MY SOCIAL ANXIETY SAYS NO

Everything Whale Be Okay

life is tough but so are you

Mentally checked out

in my healing era

I came. I saw. I had anxiety. I left.

It's OK to
be sad and
not know
why.

sometimes
i feel
OK
500 g.

Book: ON
World: OFF

i am healing every day

Anxious
But Cute

Embracing
My
Healing
Journey

MY HAPPY PILLS

mental health matters

I've Survived Too Many Storms To Be Bothered By Raindrops.